Olive Owl

What a hoot!

Barry Tranter

nosy crow

Emma Tranter

Owls can be found in almost every country in the world.

Female barn owls have spotty chests.

There are about 200 different types of owl. Olive is a barn owl.

Meet Olive. Olive is an owl. Here she is sitting on a branch. She loves being high up in the treetops.

Hello, I'm Olive. Nice to meet you!

Barn owls make loud screeching noises.

Barn owls like Olive have flat, heart-shaped faces.

During the daytime, Olive stays fast asleep . . .

Most owls sleep standing up.

Zzzzzz . . .

Animals that sleep in the day and come out at night are nocturnal.

. . . but when evening comes, she wakes up and takes a good look around. She has a busy night ahead of her!

Time to get up!

Owls can't move their eyes, so they turn their heads to look around them.

An owl can swivel its head nearly all the way around – it can even look straight behind its back!

Like most birds, Olive gets around by flying.
But Olive has a secret . . .

Owls have special soft, fluffy feathers so they can fly very quietly.

Sssssshhhhhh!

Owls even have feathery toes!

She is almost completely silent when she flies.
This means she can sneak up on her dinner!

Whilst flying, owls can hover just above the ground.

A barn owl's open wings are wider than a five-year-old's outstretched arms.

When Olive is hungry, she looks for small animals like mice, rats, frogs, voles and shrews.

Owls don't have teeth so they swallow their food whole or tear it into chunks with their beaks.

When hunting, owls use their ears more than their eyes.

Barn owls get most of the water they need from their food.

As soon as she spots something tasty, Olive swoops down and quickly snatches it up in her long, sharp talons. Then she swallows it whole.

A barn owl can eat up to 1,000 mice a year.

Ooh yum, a juicy rat!

Owls spit out the bones and fur they've swallowed in small lumps called pellets.

Life can be hard for Olive. She can't hunt when it's raining because her soft, fluffy feathers aren't waterproof.

I'm hungry . . .

If it rains for a few days, owls can get very hungry!

Snowy weather is not such a problem – owls can hear their prey even under the snow!

If it rains for long enough, Olive has to hunt in the day. When that happens, other birds can group together and chase her away from their chicks. Poor Olive!

I'm getting out of here!

Ravens and crows are most likely to attack owls.

When a group of other birds attack owls, it is called mobbing.

When Olive is one year old, she is ready to find a mate. She listens out for calls from male owls.

Barn owls nest inside trees, old barns, caves and even in hay stacks.

Who shall I choose?

Screeech!

Once she has chosen a male, Olive joins him in the nesting site he's found.

Screeech!

Screeech!

Screeech!

Many owls stay with the same mate for life.

Barn owls often nest in buildings like barns – in fact that's how they got their name!

If two females go to the same male, he will choose the one with the spottiest tummy!

Olive chooses a male called Oscar to be her mate. He has found a tree hollow – a great spot to raise a family. Oscar chases Olive through the air before they go to their tree.

Hello there, I'm Oscar!

Chase me.

The male owl chases the female, twisting and turning in the air.

Before mating, owls get to know one another – this is called courtship.

Over the next few days, Oscar brings Olive gifts of food and they cuddle together.

I really like you, Oscar.

I like you, too.

During courtship, owls clean each other and rub cheeks.

Sometimes owls make soft chuckling sounds to each other.

Oscar hunts from dusk until dawn . . .

I must get some more food.

. . . and brings the food he finds to Olive.

Olive lays one egg every two to three days.
She can lay up to 10 eggs.

Owls usually lay their eggs in late spring.

Female birds keep their eggs warm under their tummies.

After about a month, Olive's eggs start to hatch and tiny, pink chicks come out.
A baby owl is called an owlet.

An owlet is born with a special egg tooth on its beak, which helps it to break out of its eggshell.

When it first hatches, an owlet is naked, blind and helpless.

At ten days old, an owlet starts to grow its first feathers, called down.

An owlet grows very quickly, and is soon covered in thick, fluffy feathers.

By about two weeks, an owlet has grown thick feathers to keep warm.

I can swallow a whole mouse already!

At six weeks old, an owlet's adult feathers can be seen underneath its down.

At first, Olive stays with the chicks day and night while Oscar brings back food for the whole family.

When the owlets are strong enough, Olive joins Oscar and helps him hunt for food.

A young barn owlet can eat its own weight in food every night!

After lots of hopping and flapping, at around eight weeks old, the owlets are finally brave enough to try flying.

You first.

I'll watch from here.

Young birds learning to fly are known as fledglings.

Soon they learn to hunt and care for themselves, too.

Owlets stay close to the nest for a few months after learning how to fly.

Wheeeee!

Even when they can fly, owlets sometimes return to their mum and dad for food.

Meet Opal, Olive's daughter.
Here she is sitting on a branch.
She loves being high up in the treetops.

Hello, I'm Opal.
Nice to meet you!

Barn owls can live for up to 20 years!

Owls spend a lot of time roosting, which means resting in a nice, safe place.

Most owls live alone or with one mate.

The life cycle of an owl

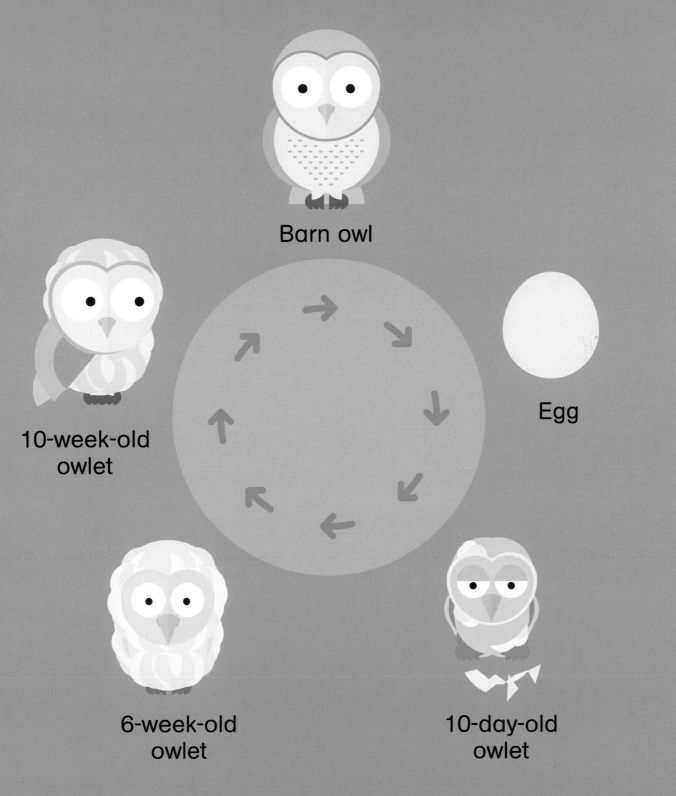

Barn owl

Egg

10-week-old owlet

6-week-old owlet

10-day-old owlet

rounds

whose real-life stories start where they end which is why they are called Rounds is a series of circular characters

Rounds is a series of circular characters whose real-life stories start where they end which is why they are called